Intelligent Investor

2 Manuscripts - Forex Trading, Trading Analysis

Michael Ross

Table of Contents

Forex Trading

Trading Analysis

Forex Trading

--- ❧❧❧ ---

*PRACTICAL GUIDE to Dominate
the Market: Strategies for Beginners,
the Psychology to have Costant Results,
Tips & Tricks*

Michael Ross

Introduction

C ongratulations on downloading this book and thank you for doing so.

Money does not just drive the economy; it keeps everything in business. When you engage in forex trading, you deal with different currencies in the world. Many people want to learn how to trade currencies effectively but do not know how to start. This book was written not just to teach you how to trade currencies, but how you can do it effectively and in a way that allows you to rake in profits. The following chapters will teach you the "ins and outs" of forex trading:

Chapter 1 talks about the basics of forex trading to give you a good understanding of what forex is all about.

Chapter 2 discusses the advantages and disadvantages of forex trading.

Chapter 3 lays down the set of criteria to look for in a forex trading broker.

Chapter 4 reveals the powerful forex trading strategies that you can use to significantly increase your chances of success.

Chapter 5 talks about the best forex trading practices.

There are plenty of books on this subject on the market, thanks again for choosing this one! Every effort was made to ensure it is full of as much useful information as possible. Please enjoy!

Chapter 1:
Forex Trading 101

What is *forex*?

Forex, also referred to as *foreign exchange* or *currency trading*, or simply *FX*, is the activity of trading currencies. This is important as it is what keeps businesses alive. It is also a driving force in the economy. Here is a simple example: Let us say that you visit India, you cannot pay the stores there in USD. What you need to do is to convert your USD into Indian rupees, the official currency in India. In the same way, the merchant has to pay using the right currency. In the given example, if the merchant gets his products in India, then he will most likely pay using the local currency; however, if he imports his products, then he will have to pay using the acceptable currency, which is probably the local currency of his supplier. As you can see, when it comes to business, there is a need to exchange one currency to another. This makes the FX market the largest and most liquid financial market in the world.

The world's currencies are traded on the forex market. It should be noted that the forex market is decentralized. Hence, do not expect to find a central marketplace. In fact, it does not even have a physical location. The trades happen online across a wide network of computers. If you want to trade currencies, then you simply have to access the Internet. Therefore, it is possible for you to engage in FX in the comfort of your home. As for the schedule, the market is open from Sunday (5PM EST) to Friday (4PM EST). It is noteworthy that the forex market is a continuously moving market, so you should keep a close eye on it.

The forex market can be classified into two groups: The interbank market and the over-the-counter (OTC) market. The interbank market is the market where banks trade, while the OTC market is where the regular traders engage in foreign currency trading. It is also worth noting that among the different currencies in the market, it is the USD that is mostly traded. 80% of all trades in the market include the USD.

The FX market is very active, which makes it a good choice for traders. However, it is also challenging to invest in currencies. It is not a secret that there are traders who lose their money in the FX market quickly. However, for those who know what they are doing, the traders who take the time and efforts to research and analyze the market, the FX market can be a goldmine of profits.

Why trade currencies?

So, why would you want to trade currencies? Well, engaging in FX is one of the best ways to make a profit. There are forex traders who are able to quit their day job and become full-time traders. You might be wondering just how much can you earn trading currencies? You can earn anything from a few dollars up to hundreds, thousands, and even millions in profit. The sky is the limit. However, trading currencies is also a kind of investment. Just like any other investment, there is also the risk that you might lose your money. In fact, if you do not understand what you are doing, then you will most likely lose your money. This is why it is important to first gain the right knowledge before you actually start trading currencies.

Forex pairs

When you trade currencies, it is a must that you understand what forex pairs are. They are the currencies that are traded. Major currency pairs in the market are the following:

EUR/USD

GBP/USD

USD/JPY

USD/CHF

USD/CAD

AUD/USD

There are also pairs that are not traded against the USD, so they comprise minor pairs. They are still liquid, but just not as highly liquid as the pairs that involve the USD. The minor pairs are:

GBP/JPY

EUR/GBP

EUR/CHF

Reading forex pairs correctly is important to a trader. Take note that in every pair, there are two currencies involved. Let us take the currency pair EUR/USD as an example. In a pair, there is the base currency and the quote currency. The base currency is the first currency in a pair. In the given example, it is the EUR. It is also called as *bid price*. The second currency is known as the *quote price*. In our example, it is the USD.

When trading currencies, there is a number after the pair. For example, it can be something like this: EUR/USD 1.25. Take note that the base currency, which in this case is the EUR, is always equals to 1. Therefore, you can view it as EUR 1/USD 1.25. This signifies that 1 EUR is equivalent to 1.25 USD.

Now, what if you want to use USD as your base currency? In forex convention, it will then look like this: USD/EUR 0.80. Be careful not to just switch the two currencies and their values. Instead, you have to divide the base currency by the quote currency. Although they may seem different, their mathematical relation remains the same. If you divide 1 by 0.80, you will get back to the value of 1.25.

Ask and bid

Let us now discuss the ask and bid price. Here is an example: EUR/USD = 1.3500/06. In practice, the difference between the ask price and the bid price is only a small amount. 1.3500/06 means 1.3500/1.3506. As you can see, there is a difference of 6 pips. For convenience, only the last two digits are written (06). Now, let me clarify a common misunderstanding. In forex trading, the bid price does not refer to the price that you offer to purchase a certain currency. Rather, this should be taken from the perspective of your broker. To earn a profit, a broker would ask higher than his bid price. As you can see, the difference between the bid and ask price is the profit that a broker makes from a transaction. It is referred to as a *spread*.

Types of orders

Knowing the type of order to give to your broker is important so that you can control how you enter and exit the market. If you want a successful career as a trader, then you should understand the different types of orders:

- Market order- This is the most common type of order that is used. It is an order to the broker to buy or sell a currency pair at the best price possible. This takes place in an instant and is made by the broker. If you want to enter the market quickly, then a market order is the way to go.

- Entry order- This is like a market order; the difference is that you get to enter the market only when the price of a currency pair reaches a certain point. You do not have to monitor the price of a currency pair all day long. You can set an entry price, and once the price of a currency pair reaches that entry point, then your broker will execute a buy order in your favor.

- Limit order- A limit order is used as an exit strategy. This order tells your broker to buy/sell a specific number of units of a currency pair at a specified value. If you are in a long position, then your limit order should be greater than the current price of a currency pair. If you are in a short position, then the limit order should be less than the market price. As a limit order, you set a limit line whereby a trade will be closed once it reaches that line. This can limit your losses and ensures your profits.

- Stop order- Just like a limit order, this is another exit strategy. The purpose of the stop order is to minimize your risk so as to limit your possible losses. With a stop order, a trade will close automatically once it reaches the limit that you have set. This is to avoid experiencing too much loss without having to monitor your computer all the time. If you reach your stop order, then it means that you have lost a trade, yet it is an effective way to prevent losing more.

Percentage in point

Percentage in point is commonly referred to as "pip." A pip refers to the measure of a spread. Remember that the spread refers to the difference between the bid and ask price. It is also how the broker makes money. The pip signifies a change in the value of as currency. You are probably familiar with how traders say that they want to profit by a particular number of pips, say 500 pips. What does this mean? Let us use an example: Let us assume that the price of a currency pair changes from 1.5000 to 1.5001. There is a change of 1 pip. A pip refers to the unit that the value of a currency pair changes. As a trader, you should by attention to the pip since it signifies how much you can profit or loss in a trade. As an example, let us assume that you buy the currency pair EUR/USD, you will profit if the price of EUR increases relative to the other currency in the pair, the USD. If you enter the trade and purchase EUR for $1.7600 and exit the trade at $1.7700, then you make a 100-pip profit. If the value of the pip decreases, then it will be a negative, which means a loss.

How many pips should you aim for? Well, there is no strict rule regarding this matter. It may depend on the strategy that you are using or the kind of trader that you are. Since currencies usually fluctuate slowly, the longer that you hold on to a particular currency pair, the higher is the probability that you can expect for more changes in price. For small or short trades, many are satisfied with a profit of just around 50 pips. This is a matter of personal preference. Just do what works for you. The important thing is to be in a positive profit when you finally add up everything.

Risk/Reward ratio

This is a calculation to know how much you need to risk in order to profit something. This way you will know if a certain trade is worth it or not. Here is an example: let us say that you trade with a stop loss of 13 pips and you have a take-in profit of 24 pips, then your risk-reward ratio would be 13:24. This means that you have to risk 13 pips to gain 24 pips.

The key is to look for a trade where you reward will be much higher than your risk. The most ideal is to find a trade that has a high reward and a low risk, although this is not always possible. There are no hard and fast rules as to what constitutes an ideal ratio. It will depend on the kind of trader you are and the strategy that you use, as well as your ability to manage risks. As a trader, your job is to look for a trade where the reward outweighs your risks.

Leverage

This is one of the reasons why people love to engage in forex. FX trading allows them to leverage their position. So, what does this mean? Leveraging is where you borrow money from your broker. Hence, you can invest and trade a larger amount. Of course, this translates to having a higher potential profit. The good news is that forex is known for having a high leverage. This means that even with a small margin, you can trade a high amount. The degree of leverage can vary, such as 50:1, 100:1, even 200:1. This will depend on your broker, as well as the size of your position. So, what do these numbers mean? A 50:1 leverage signifies that the minimum margin requirement is only 2% (1/50) of the total value of trade in his trading account available as cash. Accordingly, a 1:100 leverage would only require 1%, and so on. The usual leverages used as 1:50 and 1:100. A leverage of 1:200 is used normally for positions that are around $50,000 or less. In application, this means that if you intend to trade $100,000 with a margin of 1%, then you only need to risk $1,000. Although a leverage of 100:1 is risky, keep in mind that currencies do not fluctuate very high. In fact, normally, they fluctuate by less than 1% in a day.

Obviously, the main advantage of leveraging is that it allows you to have a decent trade size even if you only have a small start-up capital. And, even if you have a big fund for trading, it can further expand it, allowing you to profit even more. However, just be careful, because leveraging also has a catch. After all, no broker would lend you money just for nothing. So, what is the catch? Well, since you will be borrowing funds from your broker, you have to pay interest. You should take note of this interest since you need to pay your broker to continue making use of the leverage. Needless to say, you also have a choice not to leverage your position so that you would not worry about paying interest to your broker.

Day Trading Vs. Long-term Trading

Another important part of making a successful trade is learning how long to hold on to your position. Remember that a trade is composed of two parts: You have to enter the market (buy), and then exit the market (sell). How long you intend to hold on to your position depends on your preference. There are traders who open and close out all their positions in one trading day. This activity is known as day trading. A good thing about day trading is that you get to start with a clean slate every day. You are also not exposed to the risks of continuous decrease in the prices of currencies. By closing your positions within one trading day, you prevent yourself from continuously holding on to a losing currency pair. If you want to make money quickly, then you can try day trading. However, day traders need to be very active. Since you open and close out all positions in one trading day, you need to keep a close eye on the market. You also need to be more consistent in doing research and analysis. Day trading can also be stressful since you have to deal with a fast-paced environment. If you do not understand what you are doing, then this is a quick way to lose all of your funds. Short-term trades are also easily affected by the mere volatility of the market. Although price volatility is a normal part of the market, it can have serious effects when you do day trading.

Now, let us take a look at another kind of trading known as long-term trading. Long-term trading revolves around the buy and holds strategy. In this case, you buy a currency pair, you keep it for some time as its price increases, and then you sell it for profit. When you do long-term trading, you do not have to worry about the day-to-day volatility in the market. You also do not have to pressure yourself to make a trade every day. You are free do all the research you want and feel free to enter and exit the market as you please. Since you can hold on to a currency pair for a longer period, you can also earn a nice profit. Most long-term traders also do not make many trades. In fact, many long-term traders only make a few trades. As such, they do not have to do as much research as day traders. However, take note that this does not mean that doing research is no longer important. You still need to follow how the market moves. Long-term trading also has more chances to recover from a bad trade. Remember that the prices of currencies fluctuate continuously. Hence, just because it appears that a particular trade is at a loss does not mean that it will continue to be a losing trade. There is still a chance that it may recover and make a profit for you.

So, which kind of trading approach is better? There is no hard and fast rule on this matter. Rather, it will depend on the strategy that you use. There are those who make a profit with day trading, while there are also those who prefer to use long-term trading. Some others apply both as they see fit. This is up to you to decide. So, try what works best for you and stick to it.

Trading psychology

As a trader, it is also important that you understand trading psychology. So, what happens in the mind of a trader? When you engage in forex trading, having the right mindset is important.

- Be objective- When you work as a forex trader, there are times when you might be controlled by your emotions. Remember to always be objective. The market does not care how you feel. This is an important part of being a trader. Never allow your emotions to make decisions for you. To ensure that you are being objective, you should make sure that every decision that you make is backed up by a solid research and analysis. You must have good reasons to support your trading decisions.

- Greed- Greed has caused so many traders and gamblers to lose their money. Although it is good to have a desire to make a profit, you should not let this desire get out of control. A good way to prevent falling into this trap is by setting a clear objective and sticking to it. For example, if your objective is to earn 5% in a trade, then close your position once you reach your objective. Sometimes it is by holding on for too long to a trade that can cause you to lose money. Never allow greed to take away your profits. Exercise self-discipline.

- Focus on quality over quantity- It is very tempting to make multiple trades. Just remember to always pay attention to the quality of your trades. Make sure that every trade you make is backed up with sufficient amount of research. A common mistake is to take the profitability of some trades for granted thinking that you have many funds that you can use. Remember that it is better not to enter into any trade than to make a trade that is poorly made. It is not uncommon to find professional traders who only open a few trading positions. Remember that it is not the number of trades that you have that matters but whether or not your trades will end up in a profit.

- Panic- Panic is very common, especially for inexperienced traders. It usually takes place when the market falls unexpectedly. The tendency is that out of panic, traders will pull out of their positions which can further aggravate the situation in the market. Experienced traders know better and know that such unexpected drop in value happens from time to time, and so it no longer catches them off guard; they know that the market is volatile and so they are ready for any kind of change. Experienced traders know that no good can come from being controlled by a situation and panicking. Instead of being controlled by the situation, you should relax and take a closer look at the market. This way you will see things more clearly, and you will not respond rashly. Just because other traders are panicking does not mean that you should also do the same. A mark of a well-trained and experienced trader is the ability to remain calm despite difficult situations. When the market is in panic, it will be easy to read how the people will respond. If you remain calm and objective, you can use this situation to your advantage.

- Fear- Fear can be said to be the opposite of greed. In this case, you fail to take full advantage of a profitable position for fear that you might lose your money. The way to win against fear (and greed) is by acquiring the right knowledge. Fear often arises out of ignorance. This is another reason why doing research is very important for forex traders. It is by doing research that you can acquire the right information and help you to understand the market situation more clearly. In turn, it will allow you to make wise trading decisions. You should strike a good balance between fear and greed. To do this, you need to focus on gaining knowledge.

- Overconfidence- Being overconfident is a common yet serious blunder that you should avoid. This usually happens after you make a series of successful trades. The tendency is to get too confident and start to do less research. Remember never to be too confident. Being confident is good but being overly confident can make you lose your money. Also, being overly confident can lead to greed. As you already know, you should never submit to greed. As you can see, overconfidence in itself is not really bad. Rather, it is what you tend to do when you are overconfident that is not good. If you ever notice that you are being overconfident, then you should stop making trades and just relax. Be calm and take a closer look at the market.

- Self-control- Successful traders have a great deal of self-control. They do not allow themselves to be attached to their trades. They can even laugh at some losing trades. This is because they have already realized that in a course of a trading career, encountering losing trades is normal. They also exercise self-control at all times and refuse to submit to fear and/or greed. This is how they maintain the right mindset for trading. Of course, having self-control may not be easy, especially when you are just starting out, but it is nonetheless doable as long as you persist. It is easy to get carried away when you trade currencies, especially when your emotions start to be involved. This is not good because it prevents you from thinking clearly and objectively. Hence, it is extremely important that you learn to control yourself.

- Bias- This is another negative mindset to watch out for. Unfortunately, many traders are biased when making a trade. They simply prefer certain pairs more than others. The problem is that they have no good reason to feel this way. Just because you pick a particular pair does not mean that it has a higher chance at making a profit. You should see things fairly as they are. This is how you can come up with a good and fair decision. It is not just about what you like that matters. You need to objectively consider the situation of the market. Do not be attached to your trades and your decisions. Instead, view them as you would other people's trades. When you know that they are your own positions, there is a tendency to be biased and see them to be better than they actually are. Do not allow yourself to be attached to anything and see things as they are.

Chapter 2:
Advantages and Disadvantages

<u>Advantages</u>

- High profit- Trading currencies has a high-profit potential. In fact, there are people who have attained financial freedom by trading currencies alone. Also, since you can leverage your position, even a small investment of $100 can go a long way. But, of course, you need to know and understand what you are doing. With currency trading, you can earn even as high as 400% in a short period of time.

Compare this with trading stocks where a profit of 30% in a year is considered high. When you engage in the FX market, there is no limit to how much you can earn. Hence, if you have money to spare, it is strongly suggested that you give forex trading a try.

- Leverage- Forex trading allows you to leverage your position. As we have already discussed, by leveraging your position, you can invest a small amount of money but be able to trade with much bigger funds. Obviously, this allows you to rake in more profits. By taking advantage of leveraging, you can earn a high amount of profits by risking less money of your own. Now, if you invest a big amount, just imagine how much more you can earn. Of course, you are also free to decide not to leverage your position. This will be discussed in more detail later in the book.

- High liquidity- The forex market is known for having a high liquidity. This means that you can easily buy and sell currencies, as you can always find someone who would take the other side of a trade that you make. It is an active market, and you can buy and sell currencies at any time.

- Low cost- Unlike other investments where you will have to worry about surcharges and other fees, the costs in forex trading are normally already included in the spread. Even the retail transaction cost is also normally below 0.1%. even if you work with a big dealer, the cost is almost always less than 1%. But, of course, this will depend on the leverage that you pick. Since you do not have to worry about having to deal with different costs, you can put more focus on what really matters, and that is making profitable trading decisions.

- Round-the-clock market- When the market opens, you can be sure that it will remain open until the close of the trading week. Feel free to make trades in the morning, afternoon, evening, or at any time that you want.

- Fair market - There is no central authority that controls the FX market. Although there are things that can affect the market, they cannot control the market for an extended period of time. The market is also filled with many participants, and no one is more favored than another.

- Easy to enter- It is not hard to enter the FX market. All you need to do is to go online, make an account with a reliable broker, put even a little investment, and you can start trading. You can do all these things in the comfort of your home with just a few clicks of a mouse.

- More choices- With more than 25 currency pairs that you can choose from, you will definitely not run out of choices to trade. You will not have to worry about sitting idly as there is always an open opportunity for you to make a profit. All you need is to make the right trading decisions. Having more choices allows you to have more opportunities to make money.

- Fun- Last but not least, trading currencies can be fun. In fact, it is not uncommon for traders not to notice how time passes by as they make trades or prepare to make trades. Indeed, the activities of a forex trader can be very entertaining, interesting, and challenging, all at the same time. This is why you can find many traders who have become addicted to what they are doing.

Disadvantages

- Risky- It is true that people trade currencies to make a profit; however, it is also true that many currency traders lose their money. It is can be really risky to engage in the forex market, especially if you do not understand what you are doing. If you trade currencies without the right foundation and preparation, then you will most likely lose your money. Well-experienced traders use much caution even in opening a position, and so you should be all the more careful since you are a beginner. Also, there is no amount of research and preparation that can guarantee the return of positive profits; there are always risks involved.

- High volatility- There are many factors that affect the prices of currencies. Indeed, the forex market can be highly volatile. You can also expect unforeseeable events to take place. Unfortunately, traders cannot do anything to prevent such things from happening. When Iceland was bankrupt, traders who were holding Icelandic krona could not do anything about it. They could only watch as the price of the currency that they were holding dropped. To limit your losses, you should make sure to always do your research before you enter any trading position and always apply an effective strategy.

- Does not offer the highest return- Although you can make a high amount of profit when you trade currencies, it is true that forex trading still does not offer the highest rate of return. For example, trading binary options can give you a profit return of 90% in just a few minutes. When you trade currencies, it will take more than a day for you to earn a 90% profit. However, unlike binary options trading, forex is less risky.

- You are on your own- When you invest in stocks, you can ask for assistance from trade advisors as well as trade managers to help you come up with a sound investing/trading decision. When you trade foreign currencies, you have no one to turn to. You will have to make all the decisions by yourself. This is why it is not uncommon for new traders to lose their money. If you are just starting out, it is strongly advised that you take advantage of the demo account provided by your broker. It is a good way to be familiar with the real trading environment without risking real money.

- Difficult to predict- Although there are strategies that you can use, and although you can spend all the hours you want to predict the forex market, the fact remains that you can never have a 100% guarantee that your investment will give you a positive profit return. There are many things that can affect the price of a currency, and many of these things are outside of your control.

— Less regulated- There is no central authority that regulates the forex market. If you want to trade currencies, you will have to deal with a forex trading broker. It is important that you work only with a reliable broker. Unfortunately, there are many scammers online who want to rip you off. Since you will be relying on a broker, you will not be in total control of your trades. The takeaway message is to always be careful with choosing your forex broker.

Chapter 3:
Things to Look for in a Forex Trading

Set of Criteria to Look for in a Forex Trading Broker

Before you can start trading currencies, you need to sign up for an account with a forex trading broker. It is extremely important that you work with a reliable broker. Just a word of caution: There are many scammers online, so you need to be diligent and exercise extra caution in choosing a broker. Now, when you do a search online, you will find many forex brokers. SO, how do you identify the one that will best suit your needs? To help you choose a trustworthy broker, here are the criteria to look for:

- Ratings and reviews- Before making any real money deposit, be sure to check the latest ratings and reviews of a broker. This is easy to do. Simply use your favorite search engine, type the name of the broker in the search box and add the word "reviews." The search engine results pages (SERP) will then show you related pages. Be sure to read the reviews and ratings given to the broker from different websites. Also, do not forget to compare its reviews with the reviews given to other forex brokers. You should also pay attention to the dates when the reviews were made. If the latest reviews were made over a year ago, then you should be extra careful. It is also worth noting that the best forex brokers yesterday may no longer be the best today. After all, the management team of a broker may change at any time.

27

- Customer support- It is important that you work with a broker that has an active and reliable customer support. In the course of trading, you will definitely encounter issues, especially technical issues, from time to time. When this happens, there is no one else whom you can rely on but the broker's customer support team. You can direct your questions regarding the trading platform, technical issues, or otherwise, to customer support.

Take note of the ways that you can get in touch with customer support. Normally, there will be a page on the broker's website where you can send a message to the customer support or at least an email address that you can send a message to. Some brokers will even provide a phone number that you can call at any time, while others will allow you to have an on-page chat with the support team.

- Cost of transaction- Normally, a broker imposes its charge on the spread and no longer charges additional costs. However, some brokers make money on a commission basis by getting a percentage from the spread. Before you make any deposit, find out if the broker imposes a charge on a per-spread basis or on commission.

- Trading platform- Take note that it is your broker that will provide you with a platform that you can use to trade currencies. Your forex broker should at least provide you with graphs and related tools that you can use to make technical analysis. Although not a requirement, it is still a big plus if the platform is professionally designed as this can help set you up for better success in trading. The platform should make the experience of trading easy and convenient for you. It should enable you to trade quickly and easily with just a few clicks of the mouse. It is suggested that you take advantage of the demo account provided by your forex broker to find out if the platform is suitable for your needs and preferences.

- Banking options- Before making any real money deposit, you should take note of the banking options provided by your broker. It is not uncommon to find a broker that offers more options for making a deposit but only limited options for making a withdrawal. It is also common for brokers to request certain identity documents before they process a withdrawal. Make sure that you know these documents and that you have them in your possession. Otherwise, you run the risk of having your funds locked in your account without any way of withdrawing them. If you have concerns regarding this matter, feel free to contact the support team.

- Currency pairs available- Not all brokers offer the same number of currency pairs. Of course, the more currency pairs offered by your broker, the more choices that you will have. Your broker must at least have the major currency pairs, such as the EUR/USD, USD/JPY, USD/CHF, and GBP/USD. Of course, traders may also have a certain interest in a particular currency pair which may not even be considered as a major currency pair. In such case, the important thing is for your broker to offer the currency pair that you are interested in. Remember that a good broker will make the experience of trading currencies easy and more convenient and not the other way around.

- Bonuses- It is not uncommon for brokers to offer bonuses. Normally, brokers use bonuses to attract traders to sign up for an account with them. Accepting a bonus is a good way to earn free money that you can use for trading. However, it should be noted that before you accept any bonus or promotion, you need to read and understand the terms of accepting the said bonus. There is usually a catch involved. For example, A broker may tempt you to make a deposit by offering a bonus of 50%. This means that if you deposit $100, then you will have a total of $150 in your trading account. However, the drawback is that a forex broker will impose a wagering requirement once you accept a bonus. After all, no forex broker will just give you free money for nothing. Therefore, before you accept a bonus, make sure that you read the terms and conditions that go with it.

Chapter 4:
Powerful Forex Trading Strategies

I f you want to have continuous success with forex trading, you cannot just rely on luck. Instead, you need to learn and use effective trading strategies. It should be noted that these strategies cannot be learned just by reading about them. To learn how to use these strategies effectively, you need to practice them.

- Fundamental analysis- Investors describe fundamental analysis as the lifeblood of investment. As you can see, this is considered a very important strategy. Fundamental analysis deals with the basics or the fundamentals. The key to using this strategy is acquiring quality information. As the saying goes, "Knowledge is power." The more quality information that you have, the more likely that you can come up with the right trading decisions. When you use this strategy, you have to analyze the different factors that can affect the prices of currencies, such as the economy, market competition, latest trend, technological advancements, and market behavior, among others. Therefore, when you use this approach, you should be updated with the latest news.

  Here is an example of how you can apply fundamental analysis: Let us say that the employment rate in the United States has just increased. All other things being equal, then it is most likely that the price of the US dollar will also increase. Once you have this information, then you can take appropriate actions to take advantage of the situation.

It is also suggested that you check the record of currency inflows and outflows, which is usually published by the central bank. Fundamental analysis is probably the strategy that demands the most time and effort; however, it is also a highly effective strategy. In fact, it is so important that if you are really serious about making money with forex trading, then experts say that you should definitely learn and apply this strategy regularly. It should also be noted that this strategy can be combined with another strategy or strategies. Last but not least, keep in mind that you should focus on the quality of information over the quantity.

- Technical analysis- If you think that you are a visual type of person, then you might enjoy using technical analysis. The strategy involves analyzing graphs and charts. These visual tools show the price movements of a currency. The idea behind this strategy is that the different factors that affect a currency have their final effect on the price. For this reason, by analyzing even just the price movements, you also get to deal with all the factors affecting a specific currency. Technical analysis is like the simplified and visual version of fundamental analysis.

When you use this strategy, it is important that you learn how to identify and take advantage of patterns. But, do patterns really exist? The answer to this question is yes. In fact, even a completely random generator also creates patterns every now and then. However, you need to remember that patterns often come and go. This means that when you look at a graph or table, it does not always mean that there is a pattern to be seen. A common mistake is forcing yourself to see a pattern even when none exists. Remember that when you analyze a graph or table, you should always exercise a clear and unbiased mind.

Since forex brokers normally provide their traders with graphs and charts, this has become a usual strategy used by traders. However, even though this may seem simple, it also takes practice to learn how to use technical analysis effectively. Just like fundamental analysis, this strategy can also be combined with another strategy or strategies. In fact, many successful forex traders combine fundamental and technical analysis.

- Scalping- The aim of this strategy is to make small yet consistent profits while minimizing your risk. So, how does scalping work? As a scalper, you need to open a position and be disciplined enough to close it once you experience even a small profit. It is important that you do your research so you can identify a profitable currency to trade. Many scalpers rely on the mere volatility of the market. They know that the price of a currency pair rises and falls, so they just take advantage of it. However, merely relying on volatility alone is not enough. You need to pick the right currency pair to invest in. The best way to achieve this is by doing research.

Once you earn a small profit, you should close your position right away. A common mistake is to get greedy and continue to hold on to your position. The problem with this approach is that the volatility might work against you. Do not underestimate the volatility of the market. It is not uncommon for the price of a currency pair to experience a series of decreases. You have to be content with small gains. Even before you start using this strategy, make it clear in your mind that your objective is to earn a small profit. Do not worry; you can make other trades. Just be sure not to hold on to a position for too long. As long as you keep a position open, there is a risk that you can lose your money, so close it as soon as you realize a profit.

Since you will only earn a small profit, you will have to trade using a big amount to appreciate the small gains. So, if your account is not well funded, then this strategy might not be for you.

When you use scalping, be sure to keep a close eye on the market. If the price drops and it appears to be continuous, you might want to close out your position and just accept whatever losses you may experience. After all, there will always be risks involved regardless of how careful you may be.

- Momentum trading- This strategy takes advantage of strong price movements. When there is a strong price movement, the tendency is that it will continue for some more time. This is just enough opportunity for you to take advantage of it and make a nice profit. This approach is just like scalping in the sense that you should only aim to make a small profit. Momentum trading uses the same graphs used in technical analysis where you can observe the price movements of a currency pair. When there is a strong fluctuation in price, you cannot expect for it to correct itself quickly. The momentum of the price movement can be expected to continue for some time, and this is how you can take advantage of the situation and make a profit. If you want to use this strategy, be sure to do your research and keep a close eye on the market. Since you will be relying on the mere momentum of a price movement, you will have to act quickly. Do not underestimate the volatility of the FX market. Do not forget that this strategy relies on the momentum. Since it is just temporary trend, do not expect for it to last long. Take advantage of your position and exit the market immediately.

- Swing trading- Swing trading is a long-term strategy. This is where you hold on to a trade for a longer period. A key advantage of using this strategy is that it allows you to earn a really nice profit since you can keep a position for a much longer period. You also do not have to worry about the usual day-to-day fluctuations in the market. Of course, merely holding on to a currency pair for a long period does not guarantee you any profit. It is still important that you pick a profitable currency pair to invest in. Now, how you pick such pair is a matter of personal preference. You may want to use fundamental analysis, technical analysis, and/or others. Do what you think works for you. The important thing is to pick and invest in a profitable currency pair. It should be noted that since you will be holding on to your position for a much longer period, you need to follow the market in order to ensure the safety of your investment. If the market behavior changes unfavorably, then you might want to close your position. Just because you are making a long-term investment does not mean that you can be slack with your research. You have to be on top of your investment by following related news and the latest updates. Although swing trading is often known for allowing you to earn a high profit, this is not always the case. A high profit is possible, but it has no guarantee. In the end, it will depend on the currency pair in which you put your money. Still, earning a high amount of profit is possible. It will mostly depend on the price movement of the currency pair in the market.

- Hedging- Hedging is a protective measure against a big loss. It acts like an insurance policy in case something unexpected happens that can adversely affect your position. Although not all brokers may allow hedging, you can still find those who will allow you to hedge directly by purchasing a currency pair and at the same time placing a trade to sell the said pair. Although you may not have a net profit while both trades are open, you can still earn without having to take on additional risk simply by observing proper timing. The way a hedge protects your trade is that it allows you to open an opposite trade while you also trade the same currency pair. As a trader, you can always close your initial trade and then move on to a new trade. An advantage of hedging is that you can save your trade and even make money if the market suddenly moves against your initial position. Needless to say, if the market reverses and takes a direction that is favorable to your first trade/position, then you can place a stop on the hedging trade or simply close it, so you can easily enjoy your profits.

It is noteworthy that hedging is not advisable if you are just starting out as it is much harder to execute effectively than many other strategies. However, it is, indeed, a strategy that is definitely worth learning.

- Scaling in- The idea behind this approach is to enter a position gradually to lower your risk exposure. When you use this strategy, you will want to divide your position. For example, instead of investing a whole $100 into a single trade, you should invest in small amounts, say, start with $20. If it turns out well, then you can add another $20 or $25, and so on. This way you do not get to risk too much but still earn a profit. The drawback is that you will earn less than if you had invested the whole amount right away. By scaling in, you still earn a profit or at least minimize your losses even if the price movement suddenly becomes unfavorable. For example, if you have already profited from your first investment but the price falls after you add more funds, you will most likely end up still in a profit or at least just with a small loss. As you already know by now, it is not advisable to be too aggressive. Using this strategy is a good way to enter the market without taking on too much risk. Just like with other strategies, it is still important that you do all the necessary research to pick a profitable currency pair to invest in.

  Sometimes no matter how much you study the market, it can be hard to confirm the profitability of a position although you think that it is a good trade. This is an excellent moment for you to apply this strategy, instead of missing out on a profitable position. Just be sure to do all the necessary research to ensure that the position is really worth taking.

- Scaling out- As the name implies, it is the opposite of scaling in. if scaling in is about investing more, scaling out is closing your position gradually. This is a good strategy to use if you are confident about a particular trade or investment. So, you make a big investment right away. However, if you notice that the trade is becoming unpredictable or unfavorable, you can start to lower the amount of your investment in a trade. This is an excellent way to minimize your risk. At the same time, it allows you to keep your profits and still take advantage of the price movement with a lower risk. You can start to scale out if you start to feel less confident about a position that you have or if you simply want to be more careful after making a big investment. The volatility of the market cannot be underestimated, and many things can happen in a day. So, if you ever feel like you have to reconsider your position after you have already made an investment, then you might want to scale out.

So, how would you know if you should scale in or out? Well, it depends on how the market moves, if before making an investment you are not sure if it is a good position, then you will want to scale in gradually. If it turns out to be a highly profitable position, then you can continue to scale in. Now, if you are very confident of a position, then you can invest a big amount right away. If the position becomes doubtful or if you do not feel confident about it anymore, then you can start to scale out. By learning to scale in and/or out, you get to significantly control your exposure to risk.

- Pin bar strategy- This is a strategy that you can apply when you use technical analysis. The proper time to use this is when the price of a currency pair has become stagnant over some time. When you look at a graph, this is represented by a horizontal line. Take note that the line does not have to be completely straight: Minor fluctuations in price would be acceptable. This horizontal shows that the price has become stagnant is called a *bullish pin bar*. It will stand as a support for an impending increase in price. It should be noted that it means that there is *most probably* an increase that is going to take place; however, there is no assurance that there will indeed be any price increase. In order to increase your chances of success, you should not just rely on the graph alone. This is the best time for you to combine this strategy with fundamental analysis so that you can have a better understanding of the market.

- Averaging down- If you want to make an investment at a "bargain," price then you should learn about this strategy. This is also an excellent strategy to use if you want to earn a high profit. When you use this approach, you need to pick a currency pair whose price will most likely increase in the near future. You should then invest in this currency pair. If the price increases immediately, then you can cash out and enjoy your profit. But, if the price drops, then according to this strategy, you will have to put money into it. If the price falls again, then continue to invest even more, so on and so forth. Okay, this may seem like you are making a bad investment, but you are actually making a profitable investment. How? Just imagine how much you will earn if the price of the said currency pair is able to recover either back to its original price (the rate when you first applied this strategy) or higher. As you can see, when this happens, all the buy orders or additional investments that you have made will realize a nice profit. As you can see, this is a highly practical and profitable strategy. However, it should be noted that it is also considered an aggressive strategy, so you need to be cautious when you use this approach. There is a chance that the rate of a currency pair might not be able to recover. If this happens, you will most probably encounter a bad loss. This is why it is important that you do all the necessary research before you even start to make any trade or investment. Due to the highly aggressive nature of this strategy, it is advised that you use this strategy sparingly. Be sure to be up to date with the latest developments in the market, especially with the currency pair that you have invested in. Take note that this strategy is not just about observing a currency pair, but you also need to study the market so that you can take more appropriate actions.

- If you want a strategy that is practical and can give you a nice profit return, then you will want to master this one. Just do not forget that averaging down is also an aggressive strategy, so use it carefully. Just like with the other strategies, picking the currency pair to invest in is a crucial part of this strategy. After all, there is no way to make a profit unless you pick the right currency pair. Take as much time as you need when you do your research. Once you start to use this strategy, you should be ready to invest a significant amount of your funds.

- Forex wedge breakout- There are many breakout strategies that you can find. With this one, you need to find a wedge pattern where the price increases and decreases. However, unlike the usual wedge, you will see that the differences between the price increase and decrease diminish over time. This means that if the pattern continues, then it will be a mere horizontal line. The idea is to take advantage of this pattern before it turns into a horizontal line. Hence, you should open a position immediately after a price decrease. Take note that you should not be greedy and hold on to a position for a long time; otherwise, you will lose profit due to the volatility of the market. Be conservative and be satisfied with a small gain. Be ready to close your position once you profit by a few pips. You will most likely see a lower profit than the previous increase since the trend gradually turns into a horizontal line, but it is still a profit nonetheless.

- Conservative- This approach encourages you to be conservative when you engage in the forex market. Do not make trades that are aggressive, especially those trades that are not backed up with sufficient research. When you use this strategy, you should focus on making small but multiple successful trades. Do not focus on how much you will earn per trade. Instead, focus on how you can increase your rate of success. It is advised that you use the same amount per investment trade. Start out small. Once you have more confidence in your strategy, then you can easily increase the amount of your investment per trade. It is important that you take a conservative approach. Although there are no hard and fast rules as to what is considered conservative, many experts agree that you should keep your trade to not more than 5% of your total funds per trade. Starting out small and being conservative is also a good way to prevent your emotions from clouding your judgment. This is also a good strategy if you want to stay longer in the market. Be satisfied with small profits and aim for consistency. Once you gain more confidence, you can easily increase the amount that you invest per trade but keep in mind not to exceed the 5% ceiling per trade.

- Go with the flow- Many times, the best way to deal with the forex market is simply to go with the flow. For example, if the US market is booming, then it is a good time to invest in US dollars, especially if the economy of the paired currency does not show signs of development. When you use this strategy, it is important that you follow on the latest news as the news usually reveals important details about the market. Needless to say, you have to analyze the information that you gather. Although going with the flow can be profitable, it should be noted that you must not completely rely on what other people say about the market. To increase your chances of making a profit, you should also make your own study and analysis of the forex market.

You are not limited to the news when you use this approach. It is also suggested that you join and participate online groups and forums on forex trading. This is a good way to learn new ideas and opinions from other traders. From time to time, you will definitely find something interesting.

- Copy trade- There are brokers that offer a copy trade feature. This will allow you to copy the trades of other traders. You will be the one who will pick the trader whose trades you want to copy. When you use this strategy, you have to choose an experienced and successful trader among the majority of traders who either earn a little or even lose their investment.

A good way to do this is by checking the profile page of a trader. Once you are on his profile page, look at his success rate. If possible, view his current open positions and make your own analysis to gauge if the trader really knows what he is doing. Again, having your understanding of the forex market is still important. Once you are able to identify a really skillful and successful trader, then all it takes is a few clicks of a mouse to follow and copy all his trades.

Another way to use copy trading is by plotting the trades as well as the success rate of a certain trader. It should be noted that you will not find a trader with 100% success rate, except of course if he is just a new trader who has not yet encountered any losing trades. So, the key is to track his trades and only join him if you think that his trade is going to be successful. By doing this, you can "skip" the trades that will most probably not turn out favorably. Be careful since it is not always easy to speculate when a trader will lose or win a trade. This is a good time to make your own analysis and look for certain behavioral trading patterns. Still, it is worth noting that even though there are people who are content with copying the trades of other people, it is strongly advised that if you are serious about being a successful and professional forex trader, then you should only use this strategy sparingly. You must learn to depend on your own understanding of the market.

- Make your own- Even though there are many forex strategies that you can find, experts agree that you should learn to develop your own strategy. Take note that the best approach depends on the circumstances in the market. Hence, you have to use a strategy that is flexible and effective at the same time. You can simply modify and develop existing strategies that you already know but you are also free to come up with a strategy that is completely of your own. The strategy that you use is not as important as how much you earn from it. In the end, it is the amount of profits that you earn that matters, if any. It also does not have to be complicated to be effective. After all, trading currencies is not supposed to be a complicated activity. If you come to think about it, it is mostly just about identifying the right currency to invest in. You have to speculate whether the value of a particular currency will increase or decrease against the other currency in a pair.

Do not expect to come up with your own strategy quickly. It usually takes time to develop an effective strategy. To test how effective a strategy is, you should test it in a live market. This is a good time to use the demo account provided by your forex broker. It is also not uncommon for strategies to change just as the market also changes. Hence, if you are serious about becoming a professional forex trader, then you should be ready to continuously work on your strategy.

Chapter 5:
Best Practices

- Research- It is true that most traders do their research before they enter a trade. However, a common mistake is failing to do sufficient research. Just because you have researched the market for an hour does not mean that you are prepared to make a sound trading decision. Many professional traders spend hours every day analyzing the market, and yet they are still very careful when they enter any kind of trade. They know that a single mistake can make a big difference. Professional traders do not rely on luck. They know the importance of having quality information. This is why doing fundamental analysis is very important. If you want to be successful as a trader, then doing fundamental analysis should be a part of your day-to-day life as a forex trader.

As a rule, you should not enter any trade if you are not completely confident of your position. Remind yourself that you have no obligation to always enter into any trade. However, when you do, be sure that you are on top of it. This is the big difference between beginners and well-experienced traders. Beginners make a trade and hope to make a profit, while successful traders do so with at least 90% certainty that they will make a profit out of it. Again, the way to do this is by doing research.

There is no hard and fast rule as to what constitutes sufficient research. However, you will know if you have made enough research if you are honestly confident of your position and if you can justify it with good reasons.

- Continuous practice- To be successful in trading currencies, you cannot just rely on reading books. It is like learning a new skill. Hence, it requires continuous practice. If you are a beginner, it is advised that you should not focus on earning money immediately. Instead, you must first familiarize yourself with the actual trading environment. Again, this is an excellent opportunity for you to use the demo account provided by your FX broker. To avoid being aggressive, beginners are also advised to start small even if they have lots of funds in their account. When you deal with the forex market, you need to be extra careful. Continue to develop your strategy. Keep in mind that the FX market is a continuously evolving and moving market. As such, you also need to work on your strategy continuously.

It can be considered that your whole life as an FX trader is a long practice. Self-development simply has no end. What is important is that you take positive actions to improve yourself. Also, before you even apply any strategy, you should first practice it until you achieve mastery. Again, merely knowing a strategy is not enough. You must also practice how to apply it properly and effectively. Even if you think that you have learned a particular strategy, you should still try to develop it further. Realize that there is no end to improving your craft.

To continue learning, then you have to continue practicing. Reading books alone is not enough. When it comes to trading currencies, actual experience is necessary.

- Do not chase after your losses- This is advice that is usually given to casino gamblers. However, it also applies when you trade currencies. A quite surprising fact is that those who are well aware of this rule still violate it. How does this happen? The thing is that it can be very tempting to chase after one's losses. This usually happens after you experience a bad loss. The tendency is to want to recover what you have lost and, since you have already spent time and effort, you also want the profit. Since you can only earn a percentage of what you invest in a trade, the tendency is to suddenly take an aggressive approach. The problem here is that becoming too aggressive is also a quick way to lose all your money. Moreover, your funds will most probably not be able to handle such aggressive approach. It is tempting to chase after your losses because there is still a chance that you might be able to recover and even make a profit out of it. However, keep in mind that the risk is also high. If you do this for a long period, then you will most likely end up losing all your funds due to its highly aggressive nature. Instead of chasing more profits, expert traders suggest that you should focus on chasing after more profits. Continue to develop your strategy and become a better forex trader. Chasing after your losses leaves you no room for error since you will be spending a big part of your funds per trade. Some people would even risk their whole funds on a single trade. Again, this is highly aggressive and risky knowing that there is no amount of preparation that can give a 100% guarantee to the success of any position.

- Writing a trading journal or diary- Although this is not considered a requirement, it still helps to write your own trading journal or diary. It will allow you to view yourself from a new perspective, from a standpoint that is free from any bias and prejudice. It is also a good way to see your strengths and weaknesses more easily. Do not worry; you do not need to be a professional writer to keep a trading journal. There are only two things that you need to remember: You should be completely honest with everything that you write in your journal, and you should update your trading journal regularly.

You are free to write everything that you want that is related to forex trading. Ideally, a journal should include your reasons and objectives. You should also write about any new knowledge or realization that you encounter along the way. In the first few weeks, you might not appreciate the importance of having a journal but be persistent! After some time, you will start to appreciate it, especially when you recognize your progress or development as a trader. Your trading journal should act as a mirror of yourself as a trader, so be sure to be honest with everything that you record in your journal. If you are not fond of writing, then feel free to use a file on your computer or even your mobile phone. The important thing is to have something that you can write in and update easily. Of course, be sure that it will be safe and secure, so that you will not lose your journal. Although not all traders use a journal, it is undeniable that there are certain benefits that you can get by writing your own trading journal. To know if this is for you, then the best thing to do is to give it a try.

- Do not be an emotional trader- Although it is good to have passion for what you do, you must never allow your emotions to cloud your judgment. Do not forget that the forex market does not have any feelings. It does not care about how you feel. In fact, it does not even know you. Remain objective at all times. If you feel like your emotions are getting in the way, then stop and do not make any trade.

Before you commence a trade or enter any position, ask yourself if you have good reasons for taking that position. Be objective and make sure that every decision you make is backed up by solid research. There are no emotions in the forex market; everything is about numbers and hard facts, so be sure to always be in control of your emotions.

To avoid trading with your emotions, you should only trade with the money that you can afford to lose. This means that you should not use the money that you need to pay for your household bills and other obligations. This way, you will not be so attached to your trades but can think objectively. If, at any moment, you notice that your mind is being clouded by emotions, stop and give yourself some time until your thoughts settle down. Remember this basic rule: Only trade currencies when you can think clearly. Do not forget that the FX market is a challenging place.

- Cash out- It is not unusual to find traders who do not withdraw their profits. The reason why they do this is to grow the funds that they have in their account. After all, the bigger your funds are, the higher will also be the potential profit. Now, although this may seem practical and reasonable, you have to understand that it is still important to cash out your profits every now and then. You should understand that the only way that you can fully realize your profits is when you turn them into cash. Otherwise, it is as if you are merely using a demo account. Also, by withdrawing your profits, you can effectively minimize your risks.

Do not worry; you do not have to cash out all of your profits in one withdrawal. If you want, you can just withdraw 25% of your profits, leaving the other 75% to increase the funds that you use for trading. However, it is still beneficial to make a withdrawal every now and then.

- Professional approach- Many people start out trading as a hobby. Although there is nothing wrong with this, it is not the most recommended approach. Taking something as a mere hobby signifies lack of commitment and devotion. If you cannot give it enough time and effort, experts suggest that you should just be a part-time trader. The important thing is to always be professional in your approach.

- Take a break- The activities of a forex broker can be lots of fun, but it can also be very tiring in the long run. It is important that you give yourself time to rest. By giving your body enough time to relax and clear your mind, you will be a more effective trader. Now, when you take a break, do it completely. The best way to take a break is not to even think about forex trading at all or anything related to it. This is the best time for you to go on a vacation or at least enjoy a movie night with your family and friends. The more that you relax yourself the better. A short but complete break will allow you to focus more completely.

Do not use this as an excuse for being lazy. Before you take a break, be sure that you first put in some serious work. Taking a break is important, but do not abuse it. Only take a break if you deserve it.

Conclusion

T hanks for all the way through to the end of this book. We hope it was informative and able to provide you with all of the tools you need to achieve your goals whatever they may be.

The next step is to apply everything that you have learned and start turning the forex market into a goldmine of profit. Indeed, those who truly understand how the forex market works earn a decent income by trading currencies. In fact, there are those who have left their day job and trade full time. Although learning to trade currencies effectively is not very easy, every effort that you put into it is will be worth it.

It is not too late to make money in the forex market. This book as given you the keys that you need. It is up to you to put that new-found knowledge into actual practice.

Finally, if you found this book useful in any way, a review on Amazon is always appreciated!

Trading Analysis

----- ❧❦❧ -----

The Practical Guide to Learn Step by Step the REAL Technical Analysis

Michael Ross

Introduction

Congratulations on downloading *Trading Analysis: The Practical Guide to Learn Step by Step the REAL Technical Analysis* and thank you for doing so. When it comes to ensuring that your time in the investment markets is as productive as possible, there are fewer better ways of going about doing so than by learning to use all that technical analysis has to offer. Unfortunately, while technical analysis isn't too complicated once you get the hang of it, the barrier to entry is difficult enough to get past that most people give up before they even get started.

Difficult does not mean impossible, however, which is why the following chapters will discuss everything you need to know, not just to use technical analysis, but to achieve a level of mastery over it that many traders will never reach. First, you will learn all about the basics of technical analysis including its key components and the types of charts you will be dealing with most frequently. Next, you will learn all about the key indicators that you will need to know in order to start taking full advantage of the trends you find while watching the market. With the basics out of the way, you will then learn all about one of the most useful aspects of the market you will measure using technical analysis known as momentum as well as how to utilize it to reliably turn a profit.

From there, you will learn more about charting with candlesticks, including indicators to be on the lookout for and useful strategies to try. You will then learn about a wide variety of different technical analysis patterns that you can keep an eye out for as well as how to best profit from the results when you do so. Finally, you will learn about how to get the most out of technical analysis by paring it with fundamental analysis.

There are plenty of books on this subject on the market, thanks again for choosing this one! Every effort was made to ensure it is full of as much useful information as possible, please enjoy!

Chapter 1:
Technical Analysis Explained

When it comes to ensuring your successful trade percentage is as high as possible, regardless of what investment market you are working in, understanding where the market has been, as well as where it is going is, quite naturally, extremely important. Technical analysis is just the tool for the job as it allows you to study past market trends in hopes of predicting future ones.

Technical analysis is for you if you enjoy the idea of determining likely future performance based on previous currency or currency pair price movements without having to dig through all of the paperwork that is associated with fundamental analysis. While the past will never be able to completely predict the future with perfect clarity, when it is combined with an understanding of market mentality it can be an effective way to generate accurate predictions as long as you understand its shortcomings.

Price charts

The key to unlocking everything that technical analysis can do lies in the price chart which is a standard chart with an x and a y axis. The price is measured via the vertical axis and the time is measured on the horizontal axis. There are numerous different types of price charts out there, each with its own set of proponents; some of these charts include the line chart, the tick chart, the candlestick chart, the Heikin-Ashi chart, the bar chart, the Kagi chart and the Renko chart. However, the ones you are going to be dealing with the most are likely going to be the point and click chart, the line chart, the candlestick chart and the bar chart.

Line chart: Of all the types of charts that are out there, the line chart is the simplest to use because it only presents a small slice of the potential information you will get from most other types of charts. Specifically, they show the closing price of the underlying asset you are following for a fixed period of time. The titular lines are formed when the closing price points are connected with a line. When reading a line chart, you will need to keep in mind that it is not able to show a visual range that the points reached which means you won't be privy to either opening or closing price details. Even so, this chart still has its uses as it removes all the noise from the market and only focuses on a single band of facts which is why it is commonly used by technical traders of all skill levels.

Bar chart: A bar chart takes the information that can be found in a line chart and expands upon it in a number of interesting ways. For starters, the chart is made using a number of vertical lines that provide information on various data points. The top and bottom of the line can then be thought of as the high and low of the trading timeframe respectively while the closing price is also indicated with a dash on the right side of the bar. Additionally, the point where the price opens is marked with a dash on the left side of the bar. If the opening price is lower than the closing price, then the bar will be shaded black and if the opposite is true the bar will be either shaded in red or will be clear depending on the trading software you are using.

Candlestick chart: A candlestick chart is similar to a bar chart, despite presenting its information quite differently. For starters, the two charts both begin with a vertical line that shows the trading range for a set period of time. From there, however, a wide bar forms in the candlestick chart along the vertical line which also shows how much difference the price saw between the closing and opening points.

The candle will also be colored in, though these colors are not standardized in any real way. There will always be a pair of colors that indicate days where the outcome is positive and days where the outcome is negative. If the price of the currency increases over the predetermined time period and ends above the opening price, then the bar is often either clear or white and if the price has dropped and stayed there then the bar is often red or black. Finally, if the price ended at a point higher than it did 24 hours prior, but still below the point it started at then it will be typically filled with its own color as well.

Point and figure chart: While the point and figure chart isn't used as much as it once was, it has been in use for more than 100 years which means there is still plenty of use left in it. The point and figure chart is useful when you want to know the movement of prices, without worrying about volume or time spent. This makes it a pure pricing indicator without much of the noise that many other charts need to deal with. It is also useful if the other types of charts contain information that is skewing them in one way or the other.

When you first see a point and figure chart you will always be able to tell because it is comprised of lines of Xs and Os instead of points and lines. In this instance, the Xs are going to indicate periods of positive trends while Os will represent downward trends. The numbers and letters along the bottom of the chart indicate months and date estimates. Point and click charts also include a set of reversal criteria that is set by the trader looking at the chart, these criteria consider the amount the price is going to move in order for an X to become an O or vice a versa. As the trend changes, it shifts right to indicate this fact.

Range and trend

When it comes to using technical analysis effectively, one of the first things you will need to decide for yourself is if you are more interested in trading based on range or trading based on trend. These two aspects of the price of the underlying assets you are going to be watching are polar opposites of one another which means trying to commit to both will only limit your overall trading success. Both choices can lead to profitable results, though trading based on trend is generally considered the more popular of the two.

Trend: If you are interested in trading based on trend, then what you are looking to do is follow the crowd when it comes to trading and make a profit on volume along with everyone else. Trend can either more up or down, with indicators of an upward trend include above average lows with a downward trend including lower than average highs. Regardless of the trend that is occurring, the earlier that you can determine what it is, the more you can profit from it overall.

At that point, you should find holding onto your chosen position is a relatively simple matter up until the point where the trend heads back in the opposite direction. Due to the fact that a trend trader is never going to really know when it is going to reverse on them, it is important to ensure that you always use stops that are extremely controlled in order to ensure your profits don't vanish at the first signs of a reversing trend.

This type of trading is often going to generate a far greater number of losing trades than other strategies, though the individual gains are likely going to be larger in nature as well. This, in turn, means that if you do not feel as though you want to deal with a lot of risk management issues, then you will likely feel more comfortable trading based on range instead. A trade that is made based on following the trend should never be more than two percent of the total amount of capital you plan on trading with. Furthermore, it is important to keep your liquidity in mind to make sure you don't end up in over your head unexpectedly. Keep in mind that it will almost always be a better choice to take a smaller profit in the moment rather than risking it all on something that could knock you out of the game completely.

Range: If the risky nature of trend trading isn't for you, then you will likely prefer range trading instead. Range makes no distinction when it comes to the direction the underlying asset is going to move because according to range logic, it is generally going to return to its starting point. As such, it is common for range traders to actually bet on the fact that prices will move the same levels numerous times which means the skilled trader can trade these same levels time and again.

One of the biggest differences when it comes to range is the fact that the importance of finding the appropriate entry point is diminished in favor of being in early enough to still build towards a profitable trading position. Unlike with trend trading, range-based trading while also using leverage is typically considered a poor choice because if things go more than a little in the opposite direction than you are anticipating then it can become very costly, very quickly. As such, range traders typically find the most success when they start off with a bankroll that can finance the plan and hold on until it starts generating a profit.

Resistance and support

Understanding the ins and outs of support and resistance is a key part of achieving technical analysis success. Luckily, while they may seem complex at first, they will become clearer and clearer each time you put them to use, improving your skills, and your chance of success, as you do so. At its most basic, resistance can be thought of as the ceiling on the price of a particular underlying asset which means that the price will most likely not move past this point unless it is following an extremely long trend. Likewise, support is best described as the floor on the price of the underlying asset in question that the price is not going to drop past in most situations

Trendlines: While it is not uncommon for floors and ceiling to change regularly, understanding how to prepare for these lines is what separates new traders from those that have managed to last in the market for an extended period of time. Specifically, what these advanced traders have done is to learn to read trendlines, which indicate the movement the market is going to undertake. When the market is trending upward then new resistance levels form at points where the price movement starts to slow before then beginning to drown back down the trendline. This typically happens as uncertainty rises in a given market which, in turn, creates a short-term top which is a price plateau that sticks out in the overall pattern.

You will also want to start paying closer attention to the individual prices of the underlying assets that you favor as when it begins to reach the point where the trendline broadens, this is likely the point where it will turn around once more. Keep in mind that in situations like this, the trendline will lend support to a specific underlying asset for a varying period of time which means it will change very little during this time. Additionally, if the market is in a downward trend overall, then you will want to always be on the lookout for a set of peaks that form at the declining angle as well as a trendline that connects the points together. As the price gets closer to the trendline you will then want to be on the lookout for indicators that point towards selling because this is how the price was likely pushed lower in the first place as well.

Regardless of how you came about the discovery of your current levels of support and resistance, the floor and ceiling levels are going to be far more difficult for the price to break through in ranges that it has, historically, never made it into before. This means that the support and resistance levels that you come up with can make natural exit and entry points if you aren't able to come up with anything more precise.

Round price levels: When it comes to the level of resistance and support that is currently surrounding a specific underlying asset, you can generally safely assume that the prices it is going to have a hard time moving past will be round numbers. This general truth is based on the fact that numerous positions at or around relevant round numbers associated with given points of resistance or support; which, in turn, means that the price will have an even more difficult time moving past those levels.

Because of the importance of both resistance and support, there are several different types of technical indicators that have been developed in order to determine various price barriers as easily and quickly as possible. Some of which are discussed in the following chapters and while they may seem difficult at first, don't forget, slow and steady wins the race. The longer and more frequently you put them to work for you, the easier it will be to do so in the future.

Chapter 2:
Technical Indicators to Know

Many new traders who are first getting started with technical analysis often have a hard time seeing the less obvious signs that are pointing them towards various positions regarding their desired underlying assets which can lead to them missing out on key trades as the moment comes and goes without their notice. What these types of traders are often failing to take into account is that there is no single right way to trade which means you will want to learn about many different types of technical indicators if you hope to use technical analysis to bring in the profits you have always dreamed of. While there are countless types of technical indicators that you could consider, the following are the ones you should get familiar with first, before expanding your horizons as desired from there.

In order to ensure each effort is as effective as possible, however, you will want to ensure that you have a clear understanding of the benefits of the technical indicators you choose in addition to being familiar with their strengths and weaknesses. A technical indicator is any one of a variety of different metrics with a value that is directly tied to the current price of an underlying asset. The goal of all technical indicators, then, is to show the direction the price of an underlying asset is going to move as well as what the extent of that movement is likely going to be. This is done through a mixture of analyzing past patterns and determining how and when they are going to repeat themselves in the future.

The good news is that, once you have learned how to spot them, most technical indicators are fairly straightforward to pick out as they do not naturally analyze any of the fundamentals that were discussed in the previous chapter. Instead, they are focused completely on price movement which makes them especially useful in the short-term and end up losing some of their usefulness in the long-term as they typically lack the breadth of data that is required to be useful in long-term concerns. This then means that long-term investors are more likely to use technical indicators as a means of determining the right entry points to take advantage of, along with the right exit points to have in mind to avoid serious losses that were seriously preventable.

Stick with the trends

While advanced traders tend to find more success trading against the trends of the market, when you are first getting started with technical analysis it is far easier to go with the flow and trade in the direction the market is trending. This will still require some practice, however, especially if you don't already have a means of determining which trends are going to appear where. While some people will swear that a trend following tool is really all you need to get started trading successfully, in reality, they are only really helpful when it comes to helping you to determine if the right choice in the current market is to enter into a long position or if a short position is a better choice. One of the easiest, and as a result most reliable, trend measuring tools to use is what is generally referred to as the moving average crossover.

Traditional moving average: The crossover point is the place on the chart where a given underlying asset, along with the indicator you are using to track it, intersect with each other. As such, the moving average crossover is a simple way for traders to keep tabs on when the current trend might start to change. A moving average is a type of technical indicator that makes it easier for a trader to predict the price movement for a specific underlying asset by smoothing out the rough edges. It is what is known as a lagging indicator which means that it can only ever function to show you where the price has been, as opposed to where it is going.

Simple moving average: The simple moving average is actually a little more complicated than the traditional moving average because it also calculates the price of the specific underlying asset over several different timeframes before dividing the total by the number of time periods that are being used in the process. When using this process, it is common for successful traders to keep an eye out for averages in the short-term to cross the point that is greater than the existing average over an extended period of time which is a good sign that an uptrend is incoming. It is also possible for the short-term averages to generate types of support in case the price sees an unexpected pullback.

The simple moving average is also particularly useful due to the fact that they can be easily customized based on the timeframe you are following up on. The overall goal of the process is then to minimize the impact volatility has on the results. The broader the moving average timeframe you use, the more regulated the simple moving average will be just as the shorter the time the more volatile it will be.

Moving averages are an important tool to consider when it comes to finding pricing trends that could potentially shake up the current trend in a noticeable way. It can also prove useful in situations where you need to determine the overall trend the underlying asset is experiencing, with only a few additional calculations. What's more, you can also add in an additional simple moving average to cover differing timeframes which can pinpoint more complicated trends as a result.

Trend confirmation

Once you have a clear idea as to how you will determine if the underlying assets you are following are in the midst of a positive or negative trend, you will need to consider the best technical indicator for the job in order to ensure the trend will pay off as well as you might initially hope. This indicator can be especially useful because the simple moving average trends that were uncovered tend to be prone to serious periods of sporadic movement that can otherwise be difficult to properly compensate for, regardless of how far in advance you know it is coming. This means a secondary tool for trend confirmation can be useful to ensure that you don't waste time on trends that are not ultimately going to pan out.

The goal of this tool will not be to generate buy or sell signals related to the specific underlying asset you are following. Instead, it will either disagree or agree with the trend following tool that you finally decided to use. This means that when both the tools confirm the state of the market, you can more confidentially make trades that allow you to take full advantage of your certainty. The most commonly used confirmation tool is one that is referred to as the moving average convergence divergence or MACD for short. This tool measures the amount of difference that there is between two averages that have been smoothed to minimize ancillary noise.

The difference between the two results is then further smoothed by the process before then being matched against the moving average that it relates to as well. If the resulting smoothed average is still greater than the existing moving average, then you can be sure that the positive trend you were chasing actually exists. Meanwhile, if the smoothed average ends up below the existing moving average than any negative trends will be confirmed instead.

Moving Average Convergence Divergence: When it comes to confirming a potential trend, one of the most used technical indicators is the moving average convergence divergence indicator. When utilized properly, this indicator, takes the difference of two distinct averages that have already been smoothed out to minimize random noise. If this average ultimately ends up being greater than the moving average then the trend will be positive, and if it ends up being less than then the trend will be positive. The value of the MACD indicator will be 0 at the point where the averages intersect. The direction the two should cross will correlate to the trend that you are watching.

To use the MACD properly, you will need to start by determining the pair of moving averages, one shorter and one longer. Once this is completed, the MACD will take into account the value that is left over when you subtract the shorter leg from the longer leg. With this done, the results are then plotted out over 12 days and again over 26 days. If these two averages line up so that the shorter is above the longer, then you will know that the momentum is increasing, with the opposite also being true. If this is the case, then you should hold off on any serious trades in the short-term as the situation is likely going to change dramatically sooner as opposed to later.

While plotting out the MACD you will also want to plot a moving average at the same time as this will help you understand when the momentum is likely to shift. Plotting the moving average of the MACD is known as the signal line and it is an option in most trading platforms. If the MACD line cross at a point that is above the signal line, then you are looking at a bullish trend and if it crosses below then it is bearish. If the results are bullish then this is a strong indicator that the trend is going to reverse.

While this can certainly be a useful tool for those who are curious about the short-term direction that an underlying direction will soon move in, that doesn't mean it is without limitations. It has been known to generate mixed signals if the market is currently in an extremely volatile state as so many small movements at once typically result in false signals.

Furthermore, because it is a lagging indicator it can lead to several different signals over time assuming you choose an exceedingly long timeframe. Finally, it is important to keep in mind that it is not the right choice when it comes to comparing different assets that are sitting at different price points. Don't forget, it is useful when it comes to comparing moving averages, not when it comes to directly comparing underlying assets.

When you need to plot a MACD line, it is important to start with a line that clearly indicates a momentum shift. This will be called the signal line or the trigger line, but regardless it will be created if you find the moving average of the MACD itself. This line can actually be automatically plotted through most trading programs so that it shows up in the right places. If the MACD line then crosses above this signal line, then there is a strong chance that things will be bearish moving forward. Meanwhile, if it crosses below the signal line, then the trend is likely going to be bullish.

In order to successfully make a profit with a bullish MACD, you will need to have a very clear idea of what the optimum sell value is going to be as this portion of the market is still considered advisable to sell according to the moving average. When a bullish crossover occurs it typically indicates the onset of a reversal though it is still riskier to go through with such a trade than when the MACD is greater than zero.

The short term moving average is then based on the 12-day EMA while the longer moving average looks to the 26-day EMA. Assuming that this is the case, you can further assume the value of the MACD indicator is going to equal zero at the point where the two EMAs meet. The direction at which the cross-through occurs at the zero-line will determine the direction the trend is likely to continue moving in for the near future along with details you can use relating to its momentum as well.

Relative strength index: The relative strength index, or RSI, is a useful indicator when it comes to deciding how risky a specific trade is going to be. If it is used properly, it can allow you to easily determine the entry point that will provide you with the lowest overall amount of risk. Generally speaking, it will allow you to decide if an existing trend is moving in a negative or a positive direction, thus allowing you to buy into the position that is going to see the stronger move.

If you do decide to jump in early with a new position, you will want to place your first trade ASAP as this is when you will see the greatest gains if the trend continues apace. This course of action will also lead to a loss if the trend reverses in an unexpected direction. Your other choice is to instead wait for the trend to be confirmed, thus giving up some of your potential for profit in exchange for far less risk. Regardless of the choice that is right for your trading style, you will always want to consider an indicator that determines if the underlying asset in question is going to see more movement or if it is likely all tapped out when it comes to additional people to sell and or buy.

While there are numerous different indicators out that that can provide this information, the RSI is used most frequently. It is typically used to determine results for three day stretches and also measures the total number of negative and positive days before generating a value between 0 and 100. If the movement of the underlying asset in this period is generally positive, then the indicator will end up closer to 100 and if the movement is negative the result will be closer to 0. As such, if the result is close to 50 then the results are considered to be neutral.

The RSI can be especially useful when it is used to monitor oscillating indicators which often varying between differing values at the extreme ends, each of which represents a scenario in which the underlying asset in question is either going to be undersold or underbought. In this situation, the RSI will then allow you to determine which condition is currently in play along with any remaining potential that you actually end up turning a profit.

To determine the RSI, you use the following formula: 100/1+RS where RSI=100- and RS is equal to the average of the close on the days that saw an overall positive underlying asset movement divided by the average of the close on the days that saw an overall negative underlying asset movement. Typically, the indicator of a position that is overbought is 70 or higher, while the indicator of a position that is oversold is 30 or below. These can be reset to 80 and 20, respectively, if you tend to have a higher tolerance for trading risk.

If you prefer to enter after a pullback to the current price has occurred, then you may find that you are more interested in the 50-day average as you will want to take a long position if it rises above the 200-day average while at the same time the RSI is dropping. On the other hand, if you find yourself in a situation where the 50-day average drops below the 200-day average, while at the same time the RSI is rising, then you will want to take a short position related to the underlying assets in question.

When it comes to ensuring you are using the RSI as effectively as possible, many traders find that it is best to compare the results they find to those found through the use of the moving average crossovers that can be applied in the short-term. This goes for both the moving average in the 2-day and the 10-day timeframe as both can provide you with the points of crossover you are looking for to determine the likelihood that the price is going to reverse in the near future. These crossovers are likely to coincide with either the 70/30 or 80/20 spit that you established with your RSI. It can also easily be used in conjunction with any momentum-based indicators you are using in order to provide a superior means of determining both entry and exit points.

3-day RSI: The 3-day RSI is also worth considering in addition to the standard RSI as it will often show you how to maximize your profit while at the same time ensuring your risk remains at an acceptable level, whatever that ends up meaning to you. If you are holding a long position, then once the RSI moves above 70 you can assume that the best option is to take half of your profits, choose a new exit point, and split the difference when it comes to riding out the trend and playing it safe. If you are taking a short position, then you will want to look for an RSI that is lower than 30.

Tools to determine when to get while the getting is good

Finally, the last tool that you will want to consider is one that will make it easier for you to make the most profit possible while only opening yourself up to a predetermined level of risk. As you might expect, there are plenty of different tools to choose from in this category, including the 3-day RSI. For example, if you are holding a long position, then once the currency reaches as RSI of 70 or higher then you know you are likely going to want to take half of your total profits and then set a higher exit point for the remainder of your holdings. The same can be said when you are holding a short position and the RSI reaches 30.

Trailing stop: The trailing stop is a useful indicator if you are curious about the potential for profit of a given trade. Specifically, it allows you to set up precise exit points that allow for enough room for your profits to grow, without also leaving them open to the type of extra risk could allow them to grow significantly. The trailing stop is a more flexible version of the traditional stop that will automatically track the movement of any underlying assets to ensure they do not need to be reset if there is a sudden short burst of movement. Much like with all stop orders, a trailing stop will help newer traders remove all emotion from the equation by selling based on existing conditions. Instead of basing the choice on specific prices, the trailing stop works based on the amount of movement the underlying asset experiences instead. For example, if you decide to set a trailing loss at a 30 percent decrease in the current value, then short starts and fits won't be enough to trigger it unless you see 30 percent movement all at once.

Chapter 3:
Maximizing Profit with Momentum

I f you plan on using the RSI as a profitable technical trade indicator, then you are going to without a question need to understand how momentum works in order to see the best results. At its core, momentum can be thought of as the rate at which the price related to a currency or currency pair is going to change.

Determining the momentum of any currency or currency pair is as easy as watching the price and taking note of it at specific intervals. You will then need to create what is known as a momentum line for at least 10 days which can be done by simply taking the relative closing price of a given pair 10 days prior and subtracting that number by the closing price. The results of this arithmetic are then plotted as need. This idea can be expressed as the formula M=V-Vx where V is the most recent price and Vx is the preceding price.

When it comes to determining trend, momentum can be an excellent indicator to use as it can show the relative strength or weakness of the price as it is in the moment. While understanding the momentum in the moment might not seem useful right off the bat, give it time. Eventually, you will be extremely happy to know when the market is on the rise as it will give you a clearer idea as to how much time left you have if you want to make a profit from the change. Additionally, it can also be used when it comes to determining how valuable an oscillating indicator may actually be when it comes to determining the abundance of positions that are oversold or overbought. Relative strength measures a pair of different entities using what is known as the ratio line while the RSI is the most useful when it comes to deciding what caused a certain type of price action.

While it may seem confusing at first, you will likely find that it gets easier to wrap your head around as time goes on. Now if the month to month numbers increased then it is safe to assume that demand at least remained firm, if not actually increasing, which means that it is likely for prices to continue going in the direction that they are currently going as long as nothing major comes along to ultimately disrupt them.

If things went the other direction, however, especially after many months of month to month growth, then it could be cause for further investigation. While the year over year numbers would still be higher in this instance, it is in the month to month numbers that the true story can be found.

Tools for measuring momentum

When it comes to measuring momentum successfully, there are plenty of ways to do so while at the same time including the technical indicators that were discussed in the previous chapter. If you are looking to determine momentum as accurately as possible, then you will want to start with the MACD. When using the MACD to determine the momentum, you will wan tot use both the 12 and 26 period EMA to ensure the influence is on the data that has been most recently collected This is key as it will allow you to ultimately react more quickly to sudden changes in price than you would otherwise be able to.

When using the EMA in this instance, you will want to plot both it and the MACD net to the original data in order to determine the trigger line for the movement you are watching.

If you see the MACD move across the ninth line up, then you will be able to safely assume that the change is going to be positive and if it moves in the other direction then you can assume it will be negative.

MACD histogram: This fact was first plotted by a trader by the name of Thomas Aspray under the name the MACD histogram. Despite the fact that the results are a derivative of a derivative it can still be extremely accurate when it comes to determining the direction a given price is going to move. If you are planning to design your own momentum model using the MACD histogram, the following steps will make doing so much easier.

TO get started, you will need to decide what segment of the MACD you will be focusing on. If you plan on using a long position, then you will need to choose the MACD segment that comprises a full cycle as defined by the MACD histogram. This means you will need to closely watch the point where the zero line is breached on the underside of the point where the ultimate crash sees the zero-line penetrated from above. When it comes to a short, you will expect the results to be reversed.

After you have found the right MACD segment, the next step is going to locating the highest bar and then using that as a starting point when it comes to measuring its value. You will then want to determine the momentum within that segment to use as a reference point. Assuming you then have a clear idea of the direction the segment you are studying is moving in then you will want to use the momentum value to determine how the next segment is likely to move as well. If, by this point, you determine that the preceding segment was negative, then a positive trend in the current segment would be indicated if it exceeds the point of the lowest low that exists in the previous segment then there is a good chance that the signal is telling you to go long.

While this all might seem a little complicated at first, the principles at play are actually quite simple as the momentum that can be found in the histogram is useful precisely because it can provide you with clues as to the direction the market is likely to head in next. Assuming that momentum is typically going to precede price in a given direction, then this means you will want to set up in such a way that when a new price swing occurs, you will be able to get in on the peak to catch all of the resulting momentum.

This will almost always be the case as whenever there is a peak in momentum, regardless of the direction of the current trend, it is practically always going to be caused by a sudden, violent, move of the price in a singular direction. This, in turn, means that the goal will then be to determine what indications that one of these movements is likely to occur which can be done by watching for either bearish or bullish market forces that indicate a particular underlying currency is actually undervalued.

In general, these individuals are going to be early adopters when it comes to either buying or selling which means they would not be so quick to act if the current currency price didn't represent such a good value. Jumping in directly after this crowd allows you to avoid the first round of whipsaw while still making a profit by jumping in ahead of the rest of the curve.

While you can be relatively certain with your success in this scenario, assuming you can track the appropriate types of market signals, it will still be by no means a guaranteed thing. This means that there are definitely going to be instances where the strategy will likely fail due to false signals or based on underperformance that you could have in no way predicted. Above all, it will be important to always remember that just because the signals show that a signal exists, in no way guarantees how strong it is going to remain or the length of time it will last. Generally speaking, as long as you use it to determine the likely direction a trend is going to take, and not the amplitude of that trend, then momentum can be the perfect indicator when it comes to making sure your technical analysis always points you in the proper direction.

Chapter 4:
Charting with Candlesticks

Candlestick basics

C andlestick trading starts with a price bar, which is a visual representation of the movement that a particular stock has taken over a preset amount of time that can be either weekly, daily, hourly, every 30 minutes or every 5 minutes.

When it comes to creating a price bar that is truly accurate you will want to collect a few different pieces of information. First, you will want to consider the price the stock in question started the day at, the next is the amount that it peaked at, you will also want to know its overall low point, and finally, the closing price. When you plug this information into the platform that you are using you will see that the data is ultimately plotted so that it looks like a box that has been struck through with a line. The points of that line equate to the low and high price while the outer bottom and uppermost edges of the box signify the closing as well as the opening price. Stocks that ended higher than they started are colored in one color and stocks that ended lower than they started are then colored in using a separate color.

Range: The range of the candlestick can be thought of as the visual representation of the level of volatility that the market is currently facing. The greater the level of volatility, the less reliable you can expect your plans to be throughout the trading process when compared to the historical averages for the trends they are following. You can then determine the volatility of the market by looking at the size of the line in relation to the size of the box. If the volatility is already high, then the box will be large, and the line will be smaller. If the volatility is currently low, then things will be reversed.

Body: The body of the candle includes the orientation of the box in relation to the closing and opening price. If the price ends up closing higher than where it opened, you can assume the market improved overall, while the reverse will also be true. It is equally important to take note of the size of the box as a whole because the greater the size of the box, the stronger the market will remain overall. If the box ends up being so large that it completely consumes the bar, then that is a sign that the market is currently experiencing a period of neutral flux.

Split line: Once you have a firm grasp on the range as well as the body you will then want to move your attention to the top half of the line. This line portion then caps at the highpoint for the price for the day while at the same time indicating the point where the supply once more began exceeding demand, thus resulting in an overall decrease in price. This also means that the top point of the line can be thought of as the maximum amount of pressure that that the underlying stock experienced in the chosen timeframe. The lower half of the bar, meanwhile, will detail the same specifics except regarding the low for the day and the point that demand began to exceed supply.

Dual price bars: Once you decide to add a second price bar to the analysis that you are doing, you will then be able to use the dual price bars as a cornerstone that provides you with a reasonable idea of the level of movement the price is experiencing in a more practical sense than if you were looking at a single bar. The second bar will also allow you to more easily determine if what you found in the first bar is a fluke or something that is actually actionable enough to make a move on before its too late. Eventually, you will you will likely find this exceptionally useful if you need to determine if a bar is actually wide or is, in fact, average or other forms of comparison as well. This will allow you to understand the price action in a way that is more specific, and thus more effective than it would often otherwise be.

Candlestick strategies to try

Signals: First things first, you will want to target underlying assets that are already showing strong signs of trending in one direction. Besides this key fact, the bar that represents the dominant trend needs to occur in the middle of the candle and the final bar needs to close either above or below the first two candles depending on the type of trend you are watching. Once everything is in place, you will have no doubt that the trend has reversed itself.

This strategy works for numerous different timeframes as well. For example, if you are working on the five-minute chart and find an underlying asset that hits its low before sharply reversing upwards. If this is the case, and the third bar in the series closed above the highs of the other two bars then you would know that the trend has reversed. While you can move forward if the close is above the high of the middle candlestick, it is better to know what the third candle is doing for added insurance.

The exit strategy that you will want to employ for this pattern is a simply moving average, though you could use a price target if you preferred. All you need to do is watch it closely and you should be fine. Generally speaking, you can expect this pattern to have around three to one risk reward ratio for the trade you are considering. Furthermore, you will want to keep in mind that this strategy can generate returns extremely quickly, regardless of the situation you use it in which means you will need to watch your trades closely to avoid accidentally letting yourself take a loss.

The biggest downside to this type of reversal pattern is that it is possible for day traders to manipulate the data so that other traders fall into their trap. One of the main reasons that the 3-bar reversal pattern fails is when volatility isn't high enough. If the market is exceedingly choppy, then the formation you are looking for is really going to be nothing more than a pause in the overall action.

As such, it will not necessarily result in the type of swing that you are anticipating. Adding in further confirmation methods prior to choosing an entry point is sure to make avoiding false signals as easy as possible. If you buy heavily into this type of trend, then you will want to ensure that you are aware if it ends up not moving in the direction you anticipated as you will need to quickly cut your losses before it gets worse. The sooner you bail in this scenario, the sooner you can get back to looking for profitable reversals.

Hook reversal: The hook reversal pattern is most frequently found in charts with shorter timeframes. They can appear during any type of trend and are especially useful when it comes to learning about a new trend that will mark a reversal for the current status quo. This type of pattern is known to appear with a higher low as well as a lower high when compared to the candles of the previous day. You can tell this pattern from the rest because the size difference between the body of the first and second bar is quite small when compared to other, similar patterns.

If this type of forms around a trend that is positive, then the open will naturally be nearer the previous high while the low will form near the previous low. This pattern is frequently associated with other more frequently seen positions as the body of the second candle will often form with the first candle's body. The strength you can attribute to this signal will often be tied directly to the overall strength of the trend with a stronger trend naturally having a stronger signal to give off.

Abandoned baby pattern: This pattern is particularly useful when it comes to determining points that a reversal could begin within the current trend. In fact, this type of pattern is generally created via a trio of candlesticks that have a few important characteristics, the first of which is the red candle that should be quite large and clearly defined via the previous downtrend. The second bar will then have an open that is equal to its close that can be visualized as gaps bellow the close for the first bar.

The final bar will then be a white candle that is both large and has an open rate that is higher than the second bar. This bar will also represent the changing trader sentiment and, while it isn't a particularly common pattern, it can be used reliably if you are looking to predict a change to an existing downtrend. The accuracy of the signal will then be further enhanced when combined with additional technical indicators such as the MACD and RSI.

If the abandon baby pattern uncovers a bearish pattern, then it can be a useful way to determine if the existing positive trend is going to reverse, as well as a general timeline that this reversal will come to fruition. It is also a part of a trio pattern with the white candlestick forming the first portion, the second bar will then need to be the same as the middle bar of a bullish abandoned baby and the final bar will be the large red candle that will need to open below the second bar to confirm the pattern.

Outside reversal: This is a price chart pattern that can be seen when the high and low for a given day both exceed the high of the previous session's trading day. This pattern is known as an engulfing bearish pattern, assuming the second bar shows a downtrend, and an engulfing bullish pattern if the second bar is a positive pattern. This pattern is especially useful if you are looking for a means of identifying price movement for the near future in addition to getting a sneak peek at what the related trend will be. It typically occurs at the point where the first price bar drops outside the range of the previous price bar when its high is above the previous high and the low is as well. As a general rule, if the outside reversal occurs at the level of resistance then the signal is bearish and if it occurs at the support level then it is bullish.

Chapter 5:
Patterns to Know

Flag and Pennant: Both flags and pennants show retracement, that is deviations that will be visible in the short term in relation to the primary trend. Retracement results in no breakout occurring from either the resistance or support levels but this won't matter as the security will also not be following the dominant trend. The lack of breakout means this trend will be relatively short term. The resistance and support lines of the pennant occur within a larger trend and converge so precisely that they practically form a point. A flag is essentially the same except that the resistance and support lines from the flag will be essentially parallel instead.

Once you know where to find them, you will typically spot pennants and flags in the middle of the trends primary phase. They can typically last as long as two weeks before they are absorbed back into the primary trendline. Both flags and pennants tend to be associated with falling volume which means that if you see one or the other and the volume isn't moving as expected then what you are actually looking at is a reversal that is in the midst of trading the trend as opposed to retracing it.

Head Above Shoulders Formation: When it comes to indicators as to how long a given trend is likely to continue, then a grouping of three peaks within the same window of the price chart is known as the head above shoulders formation and it typically indicates a bearish trend is will continue moving forward. The peaks to either side of the main peak, the shoulders, should be somewhat smaller than the head peak and also connects to a specific price. This price is known as the neckline and if it reaches the right shoulder then the price is almost always going to noticeably decrease.

This formation typically occurs when a large group of traders is holding out for one last price increase after a long run of price for a specific security. When this occurs but the trend then changes, and the prices fall then the head above shoulders will appear. If you see the opposite, that is an inverse head above shoulders, then you know that the security holding this pattern is actually likely to soon increase in price.

Cup and handle formation: The cup and handle formation most commonly appears if a given security reaches a peak price before dropping off significantly for a prolonged amount of time. Sooner than later, however, the security will rebound, which is the perfect time to buy. This is an indicator of a trend that is rapidly rising which means you are going to want to take advantage of it as soon as possible before you miss out.

The handle will form on the cup when those who purchased the security at the previous high-water mark and couldn't wait any longer begin to sell which makes new investors interested who then begin to buy as well. This type of formation does not typically form quickly, and indeed, has been known to take a year or more to become visible.

Ideally, you will then be able to take advantage of this trend as soon as the handle starts to form. If you see the cup and handle forming, you will still want to consider any other day to day patterns that may be interfering with the overall trend as they are going to go a long way when it comes to determining the actual effectiveness of buying in at a specific point.

Gann indicators: While derided by some, Gann indicators have been used by day traders for decades, through many significant changes in the market, and remain a useful way of determining the direction an asset is likely to move in next. Gann angles are used to measure certain relevant elements including time, price and pattern which help the trader determine the past, present and future of the market and how that information will determine the future of the price.

While it is often assumed that they work the same way as trend lines, the fact of the matter is that Gann angles are somewhat different, though they can still be created automatically via many trading programs. They are a series of diagonal lines that move at a fixed rate. When held up in comparison to a trend line, a Gann angle allows the user to determine the price at a specific point in the future far more easily. This is not to say that the Gann angle will always be able to tell where the market is going to be, with ease, but it can often be used to accurately determine the relative direction and strength of a given trend.

Due to the fact that all times exist on the same line, the Gann angle can then also be used to predict resistance, support and direction strength as well as the timing on bottoms and tops as well. Gann angles are most commonly used to determine the likely resistance and support as it only requires the trade to determine the right scale of the chart and then draw in the 1x2, 1x1 and 2x1 Gann angles from the primary bottoms to the tops.

This, then, makes it easier for the trader to frame the market accurately and thus makes it easier for them to determine the way the market is moving based on that predetermined framework. Angles that indicate a positive trend indicate support and angles that include a downward trend indicate resistance. This means that by understanding the accurate angle of a chart, the trader can determine the right time to buy or sell far more easily than might otherwise be the case.

When utilizing this pattern, it is important to keep in mind the numerous different things that can happen to cause the market to change between various angles. If the market breaks a single angle, then it is likely to move onto the next as well. You can also determine both the support and resistance levels by looking at the horizontal lines that connect the various angles. If you see a greater than average number of angles clustering around a single price point, then you can expect the resistance and support at that level to play a big part in what's to come. This is especially true if you are looking at a long-term chart.

As previously mentioned, the most important Gann angles are those that are 2x1, 1x1 and 1x2. The 1x2 angle indicates that one unit of price moves for every two units of time, the 1x1 indicates that price and time move at the same rate and 2x1 indicates that two price units move for every single unit of time. Additional angles can be extrapolated following the same formula including 8x1, 4x1, 1x4 and 1x8. When it comes to performing this type of analysis it is important to always use the proper scale which is a square chart whereby the 1x1 angle moves at an angle of 45 degrees. This is a test then as only when the chart is scaled properly will the angle appear appropriately.

Along with resistance and support, these angles are also useful when it comes to providing indicators as to the strength of the market. If the 1x1 angle is fairly close to the trading trend, then this indicates that the market is likely balanced. If it is nearer to the 1 x 2 angle, then the trend is weaker than it would be at 1 x 1. If you are looking at the market from a top down perspective, then the market strength is going to be reversed which means anything lower than 1 x 1 will be the weak position.

Furthermore, Gann angles can also be useful when it comes to forecasting changes to the tops and bottoms of specific trends. This can be used to indicate that a direction change is forthcoming once the market reaches a point where price and time are moving apace. This indicator is also more likely to become visible from longer charts that start at the weekly range because it is common for charts at this timeframe to constantly have a stream of tops and bottoms incoming which makes them difficult to reliably analyze. The more tightly clustered the angles, the more believable the indicator is going to be.

Fibonacci numbers and Elliot waves

The Elliot wave principal is frequently used by professional traders as a means of analyzing cycles in the financial markets with the goal of predicting future market trends more accurately. It looks for extremes in price that includes both highs and lows, along with additional factors including investor psychology.

As you might expect from the name, the principal was developed by Ralph Elliot in the 1930s to predict the patterns that the market used most frequently. These patterns are known as Elliot waves and they are created based on the collective psyche of the relevant investors whose crowd psychology will osculate between pessimism and optimism in sequence. These sequences then manifest themselves as the trends the various markets experience.

The Elliot Principle further states that these trends are alternatively impulsive and corrective in alternating measure. Impulsive states are always sectioned into 5 individual waves which each then have their own impulsive and corrective phases. 1, 3 and 5 are all unique impulses and 2 and 4 are both retraces of waves 1 and 3 respectively.

Waves that are naturally corrective, in turn, can be broken into 3 distinct waves with a counter trend impulse present in 5 waves, then a retrace, and finally another impulse. This pattern is reversed in a bear market. Impulsive waves are more likely to move with a trend while corrective waves are likely to move the opposite direction.

Measuring degree: The patterns that make up the Elliot waves tend to coalesce most frequently between varying 3 or 5 wave structures which are the most likely to be representations of other similar waves that are occurring on a broader scale. For example, if a small five wave sequence appeared then the third, first and fifth waves will all be impulses and the remainder will be corrective. This, in turn, will lead to a second tri-wave correct sequence which you can predict beforehand if you know to look for this signal.

The full impulse pattern can include as many as 89 different waves and 55 wave corrective patterns. These cycles are classified based on the length of time they take to complete, subminuette cycles are completed in minutes, minuette cycles are finished in hours, minute cycles are completed in days, minor cycles are completed in weeks, intermediate cycles are finished in weeks or months and primary cycles can take anywhere from months to years.

Wave characteristics: Each of the three corrective waves and five dominant waves all have their own personality which can be used to identify them and understand what it means for the market in general and you specifically. The following will be true in the bull market and the reverse will be true in the bear market

Wave 1 is one of the more difficult waves to identify as the news at its inception is almost always going to be negative. This trend from a previous market is still frequently felt when it comes to earning estimates being revised based on poor performance. Likewise, the volume is likely to increase as prices rise, though not enough to alter all traders to the change. The options market is likely to experience the most volatility of all the major markets.

The second wave will then connect to the first wave bull will not extend past the point that the first wave started. The market is likely to take a bearish stance during this stage and most of the news is sure to be largely dour, though there will be positive signs from some sectors as well. Volume will generally be low, and prices may retrace to roughly 60 percent of the gains they saw during the first wave. Prices are also likely to drop at this point, though the pattern is unlikely to be visible until the third wave.

The third wave is typically the largest and most visible of the waves in this trend. The news will begin to be mostly positive and earnings estimates will begin to rise. Any corrections during this period are likely to be extremely short and minimal. Moves should have been made during wave 2 to ensure you can benefit from this wave otherwise the opportunity has likely passed. This wave is likely to extend the ratio predicted in wave one at a rate of 1.618:1.

The fourth wave is the wave that is going to be the most corrective of the various waves which means the price movement is likely to move sideways for a time. This wave is likely to retrace to around 40 percent of the third wave's value.

Volume is likely to decrease again at this stage which means it is often an ideal place to pull back to properly compensate for the potential of the fifth wave. This wave is generally characterized by a lack of progress in terms of a larger trend.

The fifth wave is then characterized by a largely positive news cycle along with a general feeling of bearishness when it comes to the current trend. This is the point where many traders actually buy in for the first time, which naturally cause their potential profits to be limited dramatically. At this point, momentum indicators will also start to show divergences and the indicators will also react by not reaching a new peak.

If, on the other hand, the pattern indicates that a corrective series of waves is forthcoming then Wave A will start during a positive news cycle that naturally writes off any dips in price as a correction to a bullish market. Wave A will also include an improvement to volume and volatility both. Wave B will then naturally see a higher reversal price point which will still correlate to the rapidly decreasing bull market. This often leads to the head and shoulders chart that was discussed above. At this point, you can expect the fundamentals to stop actively improving from this point on, though they will not yet be turning negative either.

Finally, Wave C will see prices begin to drop while volume increases. This wave is often the same size or larger than Wave A and extended to a point at least 1.618 times larger than Wave A. Remember, a true Elliot Wave will also follow three main rules, the second wave will never be larger than the first wave, wave 3 will never be smaller than wave 1 and 5 and wave 4 will rarely overlap wave 1.

Connecting to Fibonacci numbers: The Elliot Waves often return results that will have repeating numbers, it just so happens that these numbers all relate to the Fibonacci sequence which starts as follows, 0, 1, 1, 2, 3, 5, 8, 13, 21, 34, 55, 89, 144 etc. This relates to the Elliot Wave because the ratio of difference between any two related numbers in the sequence is .618, a reoccurring number in the Elliot Wave as well. Elliot discovered this number separately from Fibonacci, not finding out about the connection until after the initial work on his waves was published. This is also the number that results in the formation of a perfect spiral, such as those found in nature.

When it comes to the support and resistance levels of Elliot waves, 61.8 percent is an indication that it is likely time for you to get in on the trade in question. As an example, if an underlying security drops to this level then it is either a good time buy as the support will kick in and send it moving in the other direction. Alternately, if it tops out at this level then you know it is a good time to sell as this is typically where it will start falling once again. When performing a retracement, the Fibonacci numbers provide you with the ability to determine how much an asset moved over a specific period of time. Typically, it uses several different horizontal lines to point out support or resistance at somewhere between 23.6, 38.2, 50, 61.8 or 100 percent. When used properly they make it easier to identify the spots transactions should be started, what prices to target and what stop losses to set.

However, this does not mean that you are going to want to apply your Fibonacci retracements blindly, because doing so can lead to failure just as often as it does success. Additionally, it is important to avoid choosing inconsistent reference points which can make it easier to let mistakes affect your analysis accidentally. Specifically, you will want to avoid the common mistake of assuming the body of the candle is the wick. This is crucial as when using a retracement with the Fibonacci sequence you will always want to go wick-to-wick to ensure you determine the most accurate resistance level possible.

Furthermore, you are always going to want to keep the big picture in mind and focus on longer trends for the best results. If you fail to keep up with a broader perspective you may find that your short-term strategy is also affected which can make it more difficult for you to correctly predict momentum as well as the direction any future trends might take. Keeping the larger trends in mind will help you pick more reliable trades while also preventing you from accidentally trading against a specific trend.

It is also important to keep in mind that while a Fibonacci retracement can indicate the quality of a specific trade, they can't do so in a vacuum which means you are going to want to start with a retracement before adding other tools such as the MACD or stochastic oscillators. Moving ahead without this type of confirmation will ultimately do little to help you when it comes to improving your overall successful trade percentage. Don't forget, there is no single indicator that is going to be strong enough to warrant moving forward on a given trade without at least a little bit of double checking.

The Fibonacci retracement's other major limitation is that it doesn't work reliably for shorter timeframes because there is often too much interference from the standard volatility of the market which causes false levels of support and resistance to materialize on the chart. Furthermore, the addition of spikes and whipsaws means that it can be difficult to utilize stops effectively which then results in narrow, tight confluences.

Chapter 6:
Combining Technical and Fundamental Analysis

Whttp en it comes to analyzing the market prior to making trades, there are two types of analysis technical and fundamental. Fundamental analysis focuses on finding underlying assets that are currently undervalued, while technical analysis studies past market trends in order to predict future ones. While technical analysis can provide you with a vast amount of information on a given underlying asset, you really need to incorporate some fundamental analysis into your process to get the whole story. Using the strengths of both types of strategies makes it possible for investors to better understand the full state of the market as it currently stands and make their trades accordingly.

Two great tastes

Many parts of technical analysis pair very well with fundamental analysis, providing those who use both with a full spectrum view the market as a whole.

Volume trends: When you are researching an underlying investment, it is only natural that you would be curious to know what other investors think about it. After all, you never know when they might posses some level of additional insight into that you simply aren't privy to. Furthermore, this can help you get a jump on a new trend that few people are even aware exists.

One of the best ways to accurately gauge the currently level of market sentiment is to look to the recent levels of trading volume. Whenever you come across a large spike in trading volume it suggests that the underlying asset in question is currently garnering a large degree of attention from the trading community and that shares are being either bought, or sold, or both in large numbers.

Volume indicators are particularly popular tools with many types of traders as they can naturally help to confirm if other investors agree with the potential you see in the underlying asset in question. Generally speaking, traders tend to watch for the volume to increase as an identified trend that is rapidly gaining momentum is always going to be of interest to someone.

Likewise, an underlying asset that suddenly starts to rapidly shed volume can suggest that traders are losing interest which means a reversal is on the way. Similarly, volume indicators make it easier to trade intraday as it makes it possible for traders to pick out volume spikes which typically correspond to block trades that can also be extremely helpful when it comes to deciphering exactly when major players in the space are currently trading.

Determining movements in the short-term: While many fundamental investors typically focus on trading in the long-term, this doesn't mean they aren't still looking for the best prices possible when they buy-in or get ready to sell their positions, regardless of how long they have been holding them for. Technical analysis can be extremely useful in these situations, especially as the long-term trader won't mind holding the underlying asset until the current state of the market lines up with the most productive potential trends.

Specifically, you will often find that when a stock breaks through the 15 or 21-day moving average it will typically continue moving along the same trend for at least a short period of time. As such, this makes it a natural indicator when it comes to determining what is likely coming up in the near term. The same can be said for the 50 and 200 day moving averages when dealing with long-term breakouts as well. It shouldn't take much to understand how using both types of analysis to properly determine the right entry and exit points can be an invaluable tool when it comes to maximizing each and every trade.

Tracking longer reactions: Once fundamental analysis has determined that a specific underlying asset is worth following up on, technical analysis can prove extremely useful when it comes to charting how the underlying asset historical responds to certain types of news. The reason for this is that humanity as a whole is fond of patterns which means that when outside influences line up in a certain way, the general response is going to be the same each and every time.

As an example, if you look at the charts for various types of housing stocks, you will often see that they always react negatively if the Federal Reserve chooses to not cut interest rates when given the chance. Likewise, home improvement stocks often react the same way (poorly) to news that the housing market is taking a hit. Essentially, by analyzing historical trends through a technical lens, it makes it far easier to ballpark likely reactions to news you know, or anticipate, to be coming in the near future.

Mix with caution

Unfortunately, it isn't always smooth sailing when you mix different types of analysis, which means you will want to

...sion

...rough to the end of *Trading*
...*uide to Learn Step by Step the*
..., let's hope it was informative
...ith all of the tools you need to
...er it is that they may be. Just
...ook doesn't mean there is
...c, expanding your horizons is
...you seek. Additionally, there is
... when it comes to technical
...ald do what you can to make
...e market a top priority.

...g already and to get started
...ur everyday trading routine as
...e time to fully understand all
... indicators and charts at your
...d effort, the end result will be
...rm. As soon as you find your
...gnored were it not for technical
... hard work has likely paid for

...ed using technical analysis, it
...ystical oracle that can predict
...ear yourself of this fantasy as
...s having too much faith in
...ve you astray in the long run.
...or pattern can actually predict
...rt you to specific trends in the
...en be up to you to determine

always keep the following in mind to ensure you are helping your cause rather than hurting it by mixing fundamental and technical analysis together as one.

For starters, while it is possible to anticipate and decipher some movements based on patterns or if a particular underlying asset crossing a significant moving average, but charts often have a difficult time predicting future positive or negative fundamentals because they are so focused on the past.

Nevertheless, if you find that news leaks out about a specific company that indicates it is about to release news that indicates a positive quarter, investors still might be able to take advantage of this and the change will appear in the charts. Regardless, a simple chart cannot provide you with the long-term fundamental information you need to be truly successful such as earnings per share and cash flow.

Another important fact of the market that you will want to keep in mind is that sometimes the crowd will be wrong, plain and simple. As previously noted, there are plenty of benefits when it comes to buying into an underlying asset with upside momentum. However, it is still important to keep in mind that the crowd can be wrong which means that just because a specific underlying asset is being bought in droves this week, is no guarantee that it won't be sold just as heavily next week, leaving the owners with little to no profit to choose from. Alternately, stocks that are on no one's radar today could be all the rage next week. Not everything can be predicted.

For example, a great example of the crowd being wrong mentality can be seen in all of the money that was lost when the dotcom bubble burst in the late 1990s. While for a time the fate of every tech stock on the market seems like it could only go in a single direction, which caused many new investors to throw their money at companies that they knew nothing abou often at share prices that were already dramatically inflated fe beyond what the market would actually value the company i question at. When the bottom finally dropped out of th market, all of these companies suddenly found their stoc prices dropping to levels the market could actually suppor costing investors billions in the process.

Unfortunately, even if you had been watching the charts befor the bottom dropped out of the dotcom market, there is nc guarantee that you could have seen what was coming, and ever if you had it is unlikely you could have predicted the severity ol the change. This is because charts can't consistently forecast most macro trends. This is why a combination of fundamental and technical analysis can be so powerful, technical analysis can find patterns in existing trends, fundamental analysis can help determine which worldwide factors are going to affect the underlying asset the most.

Regardless, there is always going to be a certain degree of subjectivity when it comes to reading the charts that you decide to study the most closely. For example, if a person is risk adverse they might see the trend a stock is following and conclude that it is past caring about until the price turns around. Meanwhile, someone who is less risk adverse might still see a window of opportunity to profit from, but only if they act quickly. This is why it is important to have a clear understanding of how risk adverse you are so that you don't make the mistake of trying to listen to the advice of traders who have a completely different idea when it comes to if a given underlying asset is a risk than you do.

Ultimately, one type of analysis is going to be your primary assessment tool when it comes to finding new potentially profitable underlying assets and the second will be more for

Concl

Thank you for making it t Analysis: The Practical G REAL Technical Analysis and able to provide you v achieve your goals, whate because you've finished this nothing left to learn on the top the only way to find the mastery always something new to lear analysis, which means you sho becoming a lifelong student of tl

The next step is to stop readi adding technical analysis into yc soon as possible. While taking t of the various types of technica disposal can take serious time a more than worth in the long-te first trend that you would have i analysis, you will find that you itself several times over.

When you are first getting star can be easy to think of it as a the future. It is important to c soon as possible, however, a technical analysis is sure to dr After all, no technical indicator the future, all they can do is al market at the moment, it will t the best course of action with the information you have gathered. This should still be enough to lead you to success, however, as when it comes to finding true success in an investment market, the more information a person has, the greater their chance of success will be.

Finally, if you found this book useful in any way, a review on Amazon is always appreciated!

www.ingramcontent.com/pod-product-compliance
Lightning Source LLC
Chambersburg PA
CBHW071457210326
41597CB00018B/2582